Happiness After Horror

GIRL TRAUMATIZED BY SADISTIC STEPFATHER

GRETCHEN HENDERSON

authorHOUSE

AuthorHouse™
1663 Liberty Drive
Bloomington, IN 47403
www.authorhouse.com
Phone: 833-262-8899

Published by AuthorHouse 07/27/2020

ISBN: 978-1-7283-6673-9 (sc)
ISBN: 978-1-7283-6672-2 (hc)
ISBN: 978-1-7283-6671-5 (e)

Library of Congress Control Number: 2020912055

Print information available on the last page.

This book is printed on acid-free paper.

Chapter 1

When I was a young child, I was happy and very affectionate. Moma and Daddy were both demonstrative in their love for me. Nicknames are given to someone you love; my dad had several nicknames for me. They were Skeeter Bite, Rabbit's Foot, Woop See Doo, and Squirrel's Tail. That's a lot of love. I had a sister who was nine years older than me, but despite our age difference, she played cards and jacks with her pesty little sister and included me in a lot of her activities. This cemented little sister's devotion. When she married young, I became the only child, and as such, I was certainly spoiled.

We lived on a beautiful, spring-fed lake and had an orange grove on our property. We spent the summers at a beach house

Daddy bought for us. When I was nine months old, Moma hired a maid who was to be, among other things, a care person for me. Emma was all of four feet, eleven inches, and became a very special addition to our family.

I'm told that one day as Emma was holding my hand while walking "the toddler" in the side yard, I suddenly snatched my hand away and proceeded to walk defiantly into our grove. She rescued me before she thought I might fall. Soon after this, Emma put me in bed. At least I had my moment of freedom.

Chapter 2

My mother kept my baby bed in their room so I would be near during the night. As a two-year old, I remember being close to my loving parents and feeling comfortable and secure.

Just at dawn, I awoke with my plan to visit my friend about two blocks away. Climbing out of my baby bed in haste, I hoped that my parents would not wake up. I crept out the door and hurried down the sidewalk in my soggy, baggy diaper to Virginia's house.

It was six o'clock in the morning, and I knocked on their door. A bleary-eyed mom answered my knock.

I said, "Miz Mitchell, can Virginia come out to play?"

She replied, "Gretchen, Virginia is still asleep. Now you go on back home."

Turning away disappointed, I started down the sidewalk.

Suddenly I saw Moma coming armed with a peach tree switch. A peach tree switch can impart stings that do their job. "Owee, owee," I yowled as Moma swatted, determined to leave a definite impression.

With the swatting over, we walked back home in silence. When we finally arrived, she changed my diaper and said with a stern voice, "Don't you get out of bed again." With my legs still stinging, it seemed a good idea to stay in bed.

But being a hardheaded little girl, it wasn't long before I was enmeshed in another mischievous adventure. I never lost my stubborn streak.

Chapter 3

One of my most precious memories, starting at age two, was my daily bicycle ride with my dad. Before we hit the road, Daddy always made sure I was safe. He placed a pillow in the oversized basket, plopped me on top facing forward, and used a belt to hold me safe. We were ready to ride.

It was fun riding down the bumpy road. People would stop and say hello to Daddy. When someone asked my name, I always said, "Greddy Hendy." It was pretty good for a two-year-old named Gretchen Henderson. After a few blocks, Daddy would head home.

Daddy spent special time with me, and I loved every minute. One of the fun things he did with me was to walk with my feet

on his, and I would be walking backward. It was simple fun that was a bit scary but exciting.

These times stand tall in my memories; they were with my loving father. My only regret is that there are no photographs to show the happy child with her father. Later in life, I would make sure to document every precious memory I could.

Chapter 4

My mother was a beautiful and elegant woman, and people frequently told her so. I remember hearing these compliments, and they would also say what a pretty little girl I was. Moma would beam.

As a two-year-old, I loved watching Moma clean her face at night. She had a white cream she spread all over her face. Then, after a few minutes, she used a soft cloth to remove all the cream. I watched in awe.

When I was about three, my mother had what was seemingly a nervous breakdown, but later it proved to be the beginning of her mental illness. She started being hateful and belligerent to my dad. It was awful.

Joann and I were never victims of Moma's negative behavior. However, we couldn't help overhearing as our bedrooms were close to theirs. One time we realized from what was being shouted that Moma had a knife pointed at my dad, but he was able to calm her and recover the knife. None of these instances were brought up in our presence. In fact, things would have seemed normal had we not heard the bad sounds. Life went on.

Chapter 5

One sunshiny afternoon, my little legs were sauntering around our beach house yard. I wandered into our driveway and walked to the edge of the dirt road. As I looked down the road about fifty yards, I saw a brilliant blue-black creature. Looking more closely, I saw that it was a panther strolling away from me (thank goodness!) with his fluffy tail swishing back and forth. Being a wise little girl, I raced into the house, panting with fright.

I had no doubt about what I had seen because our beach house backed up right to the edge of a jungle. We could hear animals and their frightening sounds throughout the night. It was not my imagination that scary afternoon. After this, I was reluctant to

go very far from the house. I never had the "privilege" of seeing that beautiful creature again.

Back home, Emma would take me almost every day to swim in our crystal-clear lake with white sand. Eager swimmer that I was, I waded right in and immediately swam over my head. Then I would duck down and hold my breath, coming up gradually, only to hear Emma hollering, "Gretchen, you come in right this minute!" As I lingered, she was totally exasperated. She would scream, "Gretchen, enough is enough and too much is too much, and you is too much! Come here, now!"

I followed her up to the house, thinking only about my afternoon swim and ongoing teasing of my lovable Emma. Enough was enough.

Another favorite thing I did with my dad was accompany him on short business trips. He was an attorney and would call on elderly clients in their home. He would call me on the phone and tell me to get ready for one of his trips. I would hurry and gather a book, pillow, and a snack, and I was ready in short order. I would wait in the car while he was with his client. The reward for my patience was ice cream. I was always eager to go on one of these trips that finished with an ice cream cone.

I also loved when Daddy would take me to his office when he would return in the evening. There were three rooms: his, the secretary's, and mine, which was a small room between their offices. Daddy would supply me with everything I needed. There were pencils, a legal shorthand pad, a typewriter, and even a phone. Did I ever feel official!

One blooming summer day, I decided to go fishing. I opened a safety pin out straight and rolled up a ball of dough to place on the "hook." I raced down to our dock with my baited pole and dropped my hook into the lake. In a quick minute, I had a strike. It was a precious three-inch bluegill, and I hurried up to the house to show Emma my fine catch. Of course she fried the little bluegill and presented it to me at lunch. It was sweetly delicious, and I was satisfied with my four bites. It was a sweet victory for Gretchen.

Chapter 6

My big sister, Joann, was beautiful to my young eyes. She was everything I wanted to be. I loved the many weekends we spent at our beach house having fun sunning (my sister) and swimming (that's me!). With friends, we would body-surf, swim out to sandbars, and have diving competitions. We also loved to see who could stay under water the longest. I never won. In fact, I think I gave up first.

Back at the house, after showering, we would hurry to the kitchen to make our scrumptious bologna sandwiches. They included bologna, lettuce, tomatoes, onions, and pickles. That was about as much as two pieces of bread could handle.

About midafternoon, Joann and I would go down to the shore

in front of our house. Joann's goal was to read, and mine was to capture as many crabs as I could. Going along the shore, armed with my trusty spatula and a five-gallon pail, I would approach the crab from its back and flip him over. Then I immediately grabbed him by his flippers and carefully slung him into the pail. I considered it success when I had captured about ten crabs. They were destined to be boiled, demeated (which was a real job!), and then enjoyed as an ingredient in a delicious salad.

These were just some of the things that made being at the Atlantic Ocean so stupendous.

Chapter 7

When Joann was in junior high school, she had the cutest paper dollhouse. She painted it red and furnished it. A pad of tissues was the bed, the window curtains were flowery cotton, and the bedspread was blue cotton with ruffle trim. Cardboard made up the rest of the furniture. She had pretty feathers in a tiny vase.

This precious house had me fascinated as any four-year-old would be. After she left for school, I would sneak into her room. I changed the furniture around to suit me. I would play but had to vacate the premises before my parents got up. Joann would come home from school and scream bloody murder when she

saw the house. She would loudly threaten me and holler, "Stay out of my room or else!"

Day after day came the same routine, until one day my sister tried a new property guard to expel her pesty little sister forever. As she left for school, she would lock the door and climb out the window. My plans were thwarted since I was too little to reach her window. Big sister won the game at the time, but Gretchen was growing fast, and someday ...

Chapter 8

Every time our yardman Lonnie burned rubbish and dead leaves, I was fascinated with the pretty, silvery ashes. One day after he raked up a bunch of dead leaves and burned them, I decided to investigate the beautiful ashes. There was no fire left, so I thought that it would be safe to walk in them. Very gingerly I walked through the soft ashes and went back to my swing. Swinging was my favorite thing to do as I daydreamed the minutes by.

Gradually, my feet began to feel funny in my pretty, red sandals. Suddenly they started to sting and hurt. I hurried into the house. Emma rescued me and sat me down to remove my sandals. Much to our surprise, each foot's sole was one big blister.

We called our doctor, and he came readily, only to say I should stay in bed until the blisters recessed. He placed a calming salve on my feet and left me to heal with Emma's good care. It took several days, but then I was back out to my swing.

One day Daddy stayed home with me while my mother went shopping. He had the neatest electric exercise bike and while he was reading one of his favorite mysteries, I proceeded to climb on it and turn it on. Daddy was so engrossed in his book that he was paying no attention to my activity. I placed both feet on the handlebar as it began its cycle. At its top height, my feet slipped off and one of them got caught in the inner gear and was crushed. This instantly stopped the bicycle, but as of yet, I felt no pain.

I was scared to tell Daddy what had happened. I hesitated and very quietly said, "Daddy, something bad has happened." He looked up in shock, leaped off his bed, and rushed to me. He took one of the pedals and turned it backward. This released my foot, which began to gush blood, and then I began to feel pain.

Daddy wrapped my ankle in a towel, hurriedly picked me up, and drove to our doctor's office. Dr. Stevens said that if it had gone any deeper and gone into my tendon (Achilles' heel), I

would have been crippled for life. He gave me a shot of penicillin and put in six stitches. I would be all right.

When Moma came home, she gave me a kiss and hug and grimaced at the bandaged heel. Then she bawled Daddy out royally. We all recovered.

Maybe it will. Then

would have been complete. But I forgave me a shot of penicillin

and put in stitches. I would be all right.

When Mom came home, she gave me a kiss and hug and

grinned at the bandage. I hear. Then we howled. Daddy our

loyalty. We all recovered.

Chapter 9

I t was wartime and all the panties were dull orange, including my sister's. Little sister was conniving how to embarrass Joann in front of her boyfriend. Buddy came to visit her, and Gretchen was ready to carry out her devious escapade.

I ran into Joann's room and grabbed a pair of her panties. Out of the house I flew, waving them round and round. I passed the corner of our house and came in full view of Joann and Buddy. Was I ever successful in the embarrassment! Joann turned a bright red. The red turned to purple as she glared at me. By this time, Emma had rounded the corner and witnessed Joann's horror. Emma collapsed on the grass and made no effort to contain her

laughter. My successful escapade ended as I joined her on the grass, laughing, happy, and mission accomplished.

Joann didn't stay mad forever, and I'm so glad because I loved going to the beach with my big sister! After hours of fun in the sun and sea on Sundays, we listened to the mysteries *Inner Sanctum* and *The Shadow* on the radio.

Chapter 10

My mother's mental condition began to worsen, and she was hospitalized several times. Despite that, Moma, Joann, and I were spending a lot of time at the beach house. Joann was dating while we were there, and one of the boys she dated introduced Moma to his father. Soon after that summer, Moma told my dad that she wanted a divorce. That introduction at the beach had led to other things. Daddy was devastated because he still loved her very much, despite her illness. For the time being, I stayed with my father and Emma.

Moma went to live in our beach house. After several months, she returned, wanting me to live with her and the man she had married after only knowing him a short while. When she told me

of her plan, I became hysterical. I was horrified at the thought of leaving home and my beloved father, with whom Emma would remain. I was crying uncontrollably as my mother dragged me out to her car and "that man." I cried all the way to our beach house.

Looking back, the emotional disturbance of this time was probably the trigger to my first acquaintance with depression. It was so difficult to think of that man instead of daddy as being my mother's husband. This was tragic. Even more disturbing was the thought of Daddy being alone. This new man was the enemy who severed Moma's loyalty to her husband. Somehow, I blamed Moma for being a big part of this abominable situation.

Chapter 11

Horror began to rule my young life as I began living with my mother and stepfather. Mr. Gunter, my stepfather, was the cruelest and most despicable man I could imagine. The only thing that could have influenced Moma to marry a man like this was her mental illness. Moma had married a known gangster.

However, I have some good memories from this time. Moma was an adept seamstress and made a complete wardrobe for my little doll. She sewed a pair of pants with matching jacket and a vest with a lace blouse that had the tiniest buttonholes you can imagine. She also made a hat to match. She sewed an evening

Chapter 11

Here began to talk, my wonder it, as I began living with my mother and stepfather, Mr. Sanford, my septuplet was dire, and at most dreadful, and I could not find the only thing that could have influenced Mom to marry was a man like this was her mental illness. Mom had married a brown gangster.

However, I have some good memories from this time. Mom is who we adored. Sometimes she made a competition with the root for a birthday. She would take part in games with marching or other activities with a dice bomber that had threw some burnt holes you can imagine. She also made a harmonica. But She preserved an evening.

gown, a pinafore, a two-piece bathing suit, three dresses, and a pair of shorts that also had a shirt. There were many more items, but these are all I can recall. This was all done before her illness took her to bed most of the time.

known a puzzle, a two-piece bathing suit three dresses and a
pair of shorts that also had a shirt. There were many sweatpants
but those are all I can recall. This was all done before we all
took her to bed nestled that time.

Chapter 12

Well, back to the horror story. My mother's condition continued to worsen, and I later learned she had been given the diagnosis of paranoid schizophrenia during her last hospital stay. Although it's hard for me to believe, knowing this, I can almost understand her marrying such a despicable person. But I can't understand her destruction of a loving marriage.

Mr. Gunter spent most of his time on the road, and Moma spent most of her time in bed. I dreaded the days Mr. Gunter would return from his trips. He was revolting, and I shivered in his presence. Whenever he thought I had misbehaved, he would harshly pinch me on the inside of my thigh. I would not give him the satisfaction of knowing that he was hurting me. My mother

W ell, had to the horror story. My mother... her condition
worsened, and later learned... had been
given the diagnosis of paranoid schizophrenia during her last
hospital stay. Although it is hard for me to appreciate, knowing this
from almost infancy, and even many times such a description person...

But I can't understand her description of a loving marriage.

With Dad and apart from car... time on the road, and whom I
spent some of my first period... dreaded to for the summer
would learn from his trips. He was returning, and I shivered in
his presence. When we got to... thought I had misbehaved, he would
possibly punch me on the inside of my thigh. I would not give her
the satisfaction of knowing that he was hurting me. My mother...

was almost always in bed and was unaware of the horrendous abuse I was enduring. I did not dare complain for fear of what "he" would do.

One thing my mother absolutely demanded was my taking a two-hour nap. I began to dread these naps because my stepfather would ultimately come to my bed with evil intentions. He would get on top of me and force my mouth open. Then he would thrust his "thing" into my mouth. I felt like I was going to choke to death as he pierced my throat and pee-peed, forcing me to swallow. It was many years later that I learned the word *penis* and that it was not pee-pee that I had gagged and swallowed many times as he smothered me.

Nauseating and repulsive do not aptly describe my feelings of shame and disgust. My worsening sadness and insecurities were just the beginning of a severe depression.

Chapter 13

One precious escape was school in second grade. I was shy but content for a few short hours. Otherwise, I was safe only when Mr. Gunter was gone on his trips. Moma was becoming more removed from a sane life and began spending much of her time in bed. However, she did follow through in preparing our meals.

I remember Daddy would phone and ask me about Moma. The calls were uneasy for both of us. For Daddy because he really wanted to talk with Moma, and for me because I knew that deep inside. It hurt so much, but I was too ashamed to tell him.

Mr. Gunter was using Moma's car for his gangstering, leaving us without transportation. Our house was in the country several miles from town. When we needed groceries, I would ride my

bike with its large basket into town with a list clutched in my hand. It was a small, family-owned grocery store, and they were understanding of my mother's condition.

When our grocery bill reached a thousand dollars, the owners would call my father, and he would reimburse them. Daddy never stopped loving and caring for my mother, and he helped in every way that my mother's pride would allow.

My father was a successful attorney. After my mother's remarriage to what was a man of questionable reputation, Daddy hired a private detective to investigate Mr. Gunter and his activities. He was found to be a gangster involved deeply in gambling, prostitution, and various other illegal moneymaking schemes. Thus far, miraculously, he had evaded arrest. My dad, in his honorable way, felt no recourse but to be a silent guard and provide financial support.

One night Mr. Gunter took us out to eat. When we got home, Moma went into the house, and my friend, Mr. Frog, came jumping up. As I reached to pick him up, Mr. Gunter pulled out his pearl handled pistol and shot him. I was horrified at his absolute cruelty. Was there no end to it? He demanded that I clean up the "mess." I took a paper towel and proceeded to gather poor Mr. Frog's "parts." Then I took him out near a beautiful tree and used a spade to bury my little friend, saying a prayer.

Chapter 14

I know it seems that everything in my life was negative, but there were positive times. For instance, before my mother got so sick, she would take me down to the pier where all of my friends swam. It was an exciting time as we would swim way out to a sandbar and enjoy diving and trying to outdo each other. Those were wonderful times. Sometimes my mother would bring home one of my friends for lunch and to play. It was a relief to have fun, which was only possible because Mr. Gunter was away.

We had a cupboard in Moma's bedroom that had a curtain in front. My mother asked me to get a can of apple sauce from it, and as I pulled the curtain, a big snake stuck his head into my face. I screamed as I vaulted from the room. Moma grabbed a hammer

and beat the snake into smithereens. Was I ever impressed with Moma's braveness and her speed to get the creature!

Once, when I had a companion over to play, we decided to chop down a tree. Stealthily, I went into the garage and got the grub hoe. We argued back and forth who would use the hoe. I won. On my first thrust, the hoe bounced from the tree and landed exactly on Frank's big toe. It tore a hole in his toe and blood came gushing out while he hollered. Moma came out when she heard the screaming and loaded us into the car, after wrapping Frank's foot in a towel.

The doctor put an antibiotic salve on his toe, took several stitches, and we took Frank home. When we got there, his parents were very alarmed to see their son limp into the living room. My mother very delicately told them what had happened. Needless to say, that was Frank's last time to play with me.

One day my friend Angie and I were swimming near the pier, and a plane landed on the beach near us. When the pilot strolled by, he said, "Hello." We replied, "Will you take us up in your plane?" He said, "Why sure. But I have to eat first. Then we can go."

Well, my mother interrupted our hopes when she said I would

have to take my nap. Ugh. When I returned, the plane was gone. Angie said they had left a few minutes before I came back. Were we ever shocked when we were told that the plane had barely cleared the pier when it crashed! No one was seen around the wreckage, and as of yet, no one had come to look for the pilot. We had to leave before anything further was known. I surely felt bad about the nice pilot.

Chapter 15

Moma and I had a beautiful, black cocker spaniel with shiny, silky hair. We called him Beauty Boy. He was like a member of our family and lived in our house. Back when we moved to the beach, Beauty Boy, of course, came with us. Mr. Gunter did not like our dog. One day we let him out to potty, and when he didn't come back, I was worried. Suddenly I saw him wobbling into the driveway. When I ran to him, I was horrified to see his face. Someone had thrown what had to have been acid into his eyes. He was so weak when we picked him up to put him into the car. We drove to his veterinarian, who was alarmed when he saw his patient. He said he would treat his pain and cleanse his

eyes. We left Beauty Boy in his good and devoted care. It was so sad going home without him.

Mr. Gunter said we were moving the very next day. Unable to protest, we had to leave our friend behind. I always wondered if Mr. Gunter had tortured him with acid. I think I know the answer.

Chapter 16

Once after we moved, I was being nosey about Mr. Gunter's locked door. Since he was out of town on "business," I decided to take a look through the peephole. What I saw was staggering! On a table in the middle of the room were stacks of money, each stack at least a foot high. He was definitely involved in moneymaking rackets; my mother was married to a certified gangster. The detective had certainly been right in what he had reported to my dad!

One day when Mr. Gunter was home, he drove me to the grocers. I asked him if we could get my best friend to come home with us. He responded, "You know what you would have to do." Shivering, I knew that my friend would not be able to come with

Chapter 6

Once more approved I was being nosey about Mr. Hunter's locked door. Since he was not one to own "brasses," I dared to take a look through the peephole. What I saw was staggering. On a table in the middle of the room were stacks of money, each stack at least a foot high. He was definitely involved in something improper, so my mother was married to it. I certified he carried it... a hid certainty but not in what he had reported to V.E.

One day when Mrs. Currie was home, he drew me to the grocery. I asked him how he could get my house, and the complaints without the reschedule. You know, what you would have to do. Shivering, I knew that my friend would not be able to come with

me. Mr. Gunter, on these trips, would drive in his underwear with his thing poking out. This was an incredibly dark time, and I felt so ashamed and humiliated. It cast a shadowy pall over my existence.

We had a companion and housekeeper for Moma, and she also cooked our meals. Lola was kind, and Moma appreciated her company. My mother was still in her room most of the time. She was very generous and gave Lola some beautiful dresses. I was almost happy when it was only Moma, Lola, and me. When Mr. Gunter came home, I hated to think of our home as including this nasty so-called "human" being.

We had placed a bed and table on our side porch for Lola. The entrance door was there, and when Mr. Gunter came home, he was furious to see Moma's clothes on the porch with Lola's things. Did he think she had stolen them? He grabbed her by the arm and forced her outside, where he told her to stay until her brother could come get her. She had to wait outside for two days and a night. He forbade us to go out to her for any reason.

Mr. Gunter had the frightening habit of twirling his gun around and "playfully" pointing it at "pretend" targets. It was terrifying, and we did (almost) everything he said to do or not to

do. This was our home, but calling it that was a defamation with Mr. Gunter living there.

One night when I was asleep, I awoke to my mother screaming repeatedly. I jumped out of bed and went to their closed bedroom door. Peeking into the peephole, I saw Moma was nude and sitting on Mr. Gunter's stomach. He was slapping her face back and forth and Moma was sobbing as she screamed. I was so scared for her and myself and deeply sad to know there was nothing I could do. I reluctantly returned to my bed and spent a sleepless night. The next day, Mr. Gunter left on one of his trips and Moma stayed in her bed. Nothing was said about the night before.

Mr. Gunter took me to one of his nightclub operations. We sat down with some of his cohorts. Almost immediately, Mr. Gunter left and went upstairs. After a few minutes, we heard a loud gunshot. Then Mr. Gunter came dashing down the stairs and grabbed me on his way out. Nothing ever developed out of that shooting except that, according to my stepfather, it was suicide. I wondered if a pearl-handled gun had caused the death.

Soon after that, Mr. Gunter *thankfully* disappeared, and I was free from him. I didn't realize until much later how the years with him had damaged me. When he left, my mother's mental illness

began to worsen, and she was admitted to the hospital. I was sad about Moma's condition, but it meant that I could live with my father, and that made me happy. He had remarried, and I moved in with him and my stepmother.

Chapter 17

Despite my happiness, I was very shy; I was no longer an adventurous, confident child. One day when my daddy took me to school after being gone for over two years, I had a siege of shyness. When we came to my class door, the kids began shouting, "Gretchen's home!" I smiled very timidly but quickly became overwhelmed with fear. I asked Daddy to take me home because my shoe strap had come loose, and we left. The emotional turmoil of the past years was showing its effects. I carried much fear and sadness on my shoulders.

The next day, I decided to try my scholarly entrance again. All went well, and eventually I was happy to be back with my friends.

It didn't take long for my stepmother to reveal her jealous

and scheming nature, and we were soon alienated. My poor dad was caught in the middle, but he did his best to placate my stepmother so that I was more comfortable. Despite his efforts, I was becoming more and more insecure and depressed.

I had a friend who felt the same way. In a time of mutual despair, we decided to run away. After school was dismissed, we walked to my home to prepare (since no one would be there). We filled an empty gallon milk jug with water, and I brought along a large candy bar. So went the preparations.

We began to walk and discuss our plans. We decided that each of us would get a job. She would cook for a family, and I would mow lawns, which was my job at home. We thought we had walked several miles while we were planning because it was starting to get dark. Getting alarmed that it would be completely dark very soon, we walked back into an orange grove and came to a sand hill. We climbed to the top and planned to stay the night.

As the moonless, black night began to envelope us, we became frightened and started calling, "Help!" every few minutes. Suddenly we saw spotlights shining back and forth over the grove. We hesitated and then hurriedly climbed down and

scurried toward the lights. As we grew nearer, we realized it was a police car. Surprised at seeing us, one of the policemen quickly asked if we were all right. We were saved, thank goodness!

Later we were astounded to learn that the policemen were not trying to find us. Instead, they were searching for two escaped convicts who had been seen fleeing into the grove!

We were taken to our homes and my friend was surrounded by loving arms. Not so at my home. My father was furious with me and could hardly speak. He told me that we would "discuss" my escapade in a few days. Finally, the day came, and with my head locked between his knees, Daddy delivered a spanking that was so harsh, I am certain it hurt his hand almost as much as my bottom. Crying was a relief, and there was plenty of it.

The next day, my dad took me aside and told me how much he loved me. Forgiveness was such a comfort. Afterward, and in the days that followed, I knew a sense of loving and security. My stepmother even proclaimed her love for me.

Chapter 18

Now that I was living back with Daddy, I was able to swim in my beautiful, spring-fed lake every day. We had a boat and skiing was our favorite pursuit, especially with my friends. One day, a friend and I skipped last period and proceeded to ski. Joe was driving the boat and I was sloloming, and we were hollering about seeing an alligator. What we forgot was that our school was on a hill over the lake and the principal's office presented a full view of us as we hollered back and forth. The next day at school, the principal stopped me in the hall. With a clever look on his face, he asked me if I had been skiing lately. With that, he gave me an impish grin and went on his way. No wonder he was so well liked.

Around this time, I was "volunteered" to babysit my sister's two toddlers Friday and Saturday nights. I was to stay at Joann's for the weekend. Thus began the unwinding of love and security that I had begun to feel. I was devoted to my little niece and nephew and my sister. However, it was not home.

I began to vacillate between sheer happiness and feeling lost and no good. (Only much later did I learn that I am bipolar.) Through my junior year in high school, I was more depressed than I had ever been.

Chapter 19

After eight long years and the advent of tranquilizers, my mother was well enough to be discharged from the hospital. Moma went to live with her mother. Daddy felt strongly that my mother and grandmother needed my help, which meant that I would change schools at the beginning of my senior year. It was a hard transition, but I loved my mother and resigned to do my best. I dearly loved my grandmother, and was she ever a great cook! I can almost smell her fried chicken and chicken and dumplings. Yummmm!

Chapter 20

Shortly after I began college, I got engaged to a high school boyfriend, and we were married. I soon realized that I was not his only love, but I believed in my wedding vows and remained faithful. The years went by, and the affairs continued. My daddy knew I was unhappy and tried to help me in many ways; his love was one of the only positives I was able to see. Depression continued to consume me. Thankfully, during this time, I accepted a job as administrative assistant to the president of the university, which kept me in a partially positive state while at work. As soon as I walked back into my home, depression enveloped me.

One night I was completely consumed by depression and

ingested twenty sleeping pills. After several hours of forced sleep, I awoke, vomiting almost all of the pills I had taken. My husband rushed me to the hospital, where I was in somewhat of a drunken stupor. I answered their questions regarding an "attempted suicide" with what I hoped was a convincing denial.

After several days in the hospital, I went home with a very angry husband who was certain that I had failed at suicide. Later I began to wonder if his anger was directed at me because I had been unsuccessful.

Suffering from much stress, I returned to the office, where I was greeted happily.

Chapter 21

After several years of trying to conceal my depression, I reluctantly resigned my job. This was on a Tuesday, and the next Thursday, I awoke early in total agony and despair. Careful not to wake my husband, I slipped out to our garage and got my gun from my car. I moved deeper into the garage, and without hesitation, I aimed the gun at my forehead and fired. Much to my dismay, after the shot, I was dazed and still alive. As the blood drizzled down my forehead, my instant belief was that I would never be successful at killing myself. In a frenzied, nervous attempt at driving, my husband managed to get me to the hospital. I lay on the gurney in total exhaustion and complete disgust at my dismal, failed attempt.

The doctor said that as I fired the shot, my hand turned upward and the bullet pierced my skull, digging a bone-splintering fissure. After sewing me up, the doctor spoke quietly, saying that later I would appreciate his careful stitching because as I approached my "golden" years and began to wrinkle in the scarred area, it would seem to disappear.

I knew the depression would continue to torture me after my time in the hospital and then going home, but I was hopeful that medicine would help. It brought some measure of peace to be told I was bipolar, that it could be controlled, and that I could have a normal life.

Chapter 22

Three months later, I was still down, but the doctor decided it was time to share some surprising news with me. He told me that I had been two weeks' pregnant when I tried to end my life. My intense gloom seemed to disintegrate when I realized that I had experienced a miracle.

My daughter arrived healthy and beautiful six months later. I named her Madison Angelique and she was (and is) my adorable sunshine.

Chapter 23

Of all the horrors I have endured, the most horrific and disturbing would be what I am going to reveal to you now. I had visited my best friend and her husband and I discussed what a horrible marriage ours had become. It was so bad that our threemonth old baby girl whom we had named Madison Angelique was busy trying to count sheep and was fussy. However, it was a peaceful evening that developed into unbelievable shock. When I came home, immediately I became aware of a conversation between my husband and his mother. It was a lewd exchange between the two.

His mother began commenting to the effect that I was simply out trying to make him jealous. I opened my mouth to say, "Thanks a lot, Effie."

Seth became blind with fury probably because he realized that I had heard their dirty talk. I proceeded to go to our bedroom to dress for bed. Seth charged into the bedroom and grabbed my arm, twisting it until I was able to break his hold. I dashed to the door but was stopped by him as he slammed me against the wall. Seth began punching me in the stomach. I slid down the wall, terrified. All at once, he panted, "I'm going to kill you."

He determinately strod out of the house to get the gun from his car. Barefooted and in my pajamas, I raced out the front door. Instantly I ran for the dark orange grove across the road. Thank goodness I was out of Seth's sight.

I was about thirty yards from the road when I heard Seth's Charger speeding back and forth as he shown his spotlight toward the grove. He never saw me. After running blindly for three miles, I at last reached the country road which was my first destination, leading to my friends house.

Very cautiously I began running, terrified that any minute the Charger would come screaming into my path. In my favor, Seth did not know where my friends lived. I was heading toward their house in a frantic pace to reach salvation.

I was panting and out of breath when suddenly it dawned on me that I must look quite crazy. There I was, with wet pajama bottoms and bare feet covered with grove fertilizer and dirt. Calling on my exhausted but hale effort, braving knocked on their door. My friend Susan opened the door and to her credit she did not look surprised or upset but greeted me nicely. Obviously we began discussing appearance. However, she did not seem alarmed but insisted that I come into their family room where her husband and father were gathered. Citing my wet and dirty condition, she demanded that I join them and sit down. Uncomfortably I did so. They listened intently as I related the unbelievable events of the past few hours. With their concern obvious, Mr. Phillips volunteered to call my best friend to pick me up. Very soon she came for me and took me to their home. I repeated the total events leading up to my appearance. Susan and her husband Sam were not totally surprised since earlier that evening I had visited them and told them what bad condition

found our marriage. After I was sure Seth would have left for his office, I went home to get Madison who had been in the care of her grandmother. I called my sister to ask if Madison and I could stay with her for a while. Of course was the welcome reply. I hurriedly packed all the clothes I could along with Madison's toys and stuffed animals. I thanked Effie for her help and my daughter and I left our home for good. The next day I began divorce proceedings.

After I was free from my husband, Madison and I moved and I began work as a secretary again. I was fortunate to find a good sitter for Madison who over the years became a wonderful friend. Madison loved Mrs. Peterson and was growing to be a happy and intelligent little girl.

Chapter 24

This was our life for six years. I knew we were doing all right when Madison hugged my knees and said, "Mommy, you're a good home." Ahhhhhhhhhh. Another day she asked me something that cracked me up. "What if we had hair on our tongues and teeth on our eyeballs?" Gross but funny, and with no answer, I just laughed.

Though I had happiness in my life, I still endured occasional depression. Being bipolar, I could still succumb. Each time after struggling deeply for a few months, I was able to fight my way out of it by reminding myself of all the reasons I had to live. I was able to escape the misery by using this positive thinking along with medication.

My job was rewarding. I enjoyed being the secretary to the owner, Patrick Peterson, who became a good friend. Unknown to me, he had met a gentleman who was a widower. Patrick was impressed with John Mathers and made a suggestion to John regarding meeting me.

John began calling me every day, and I was intrigued with his dialogue. These conversations developed into his suggestion that we meet for lunch. This occurred after several weeks of talking over the phone.

After a spirited courtship of several months, we were completely enamored of each other and made plans for our marriage in two months. Thus began a vibrant and wonderful relationship lasting over forty-two years and including four children.

As I said earlier, I was determined to document all the precious memories I could. I wanted a complete library of photos. At last count, I have fifty-nine albums covering my family for forty-two years.

Chapter 25

To my great sadness, John developed Alzheimer's, and I knew it meant our time was limited. I was so grateful for my photo library because we were able to look back at our entire lives together! We spent much time with the colorful photos, and it stimulated his memory as we both enjoyed our family echoes.

After several months of suffering, my husband passed away peacefully in his sleep. All of our children were able to spend precious time with him over those months. What a glorious way to make that final journey! He is no longer in pain. Thank God.

I miss him greatly every day. Covering the wall in front of my recliner, I have eight-inch-by-ten-inch photos of my handsome

husband and beautiful family that represent every one of our years together. I'm so glad I have these pictures!

Since his death, I have continued to live at an assisted living facility. I find myself comfortably busy but also with time for my needed solitude.

Life is good.

Printed in the United States
By Bookmasters

Printed in the United States
By Bookmasters